Slowly/Sud

Allison Blevins

Library of Congress Control Number: 2021944780

Cover Image: *Lady Blue 1* by **C.R. Resetarits**

For Laura Lee Washburn

Table of Contents

I.

II.

I.

Well I use the past to make my pics and I want all of it and even you and me in candlelight on the train and every "lover" I've ever had—every friend—nothing closed out—and dogs alive and dead and people and landscapes and feeling even if it is desperate—anguished—tragic—it's all part of me and I want to confront it and sleep with it—the dreams— and paint it.

—Joan Mitchell

Season 4, Episode 11: "Delivering Baby Mason"
After Gino Severini's Femme et enfant, *1916*

I am watching a woman pull her own child from her body. *I can't believe he's all mine.* Woman folds and folds into squares, into herself, disappears. I am a kitchen yellowed tile: bacon, butter and splatter. I am stink and vinegar sting. Woman pulls her own child from her body. Woman in a luxury car, on the back of a motorcycle, pruning in the yard or tub. Folding.

I am a chair. I am leaking petals and leaves from my breast. I once slept in a motel, door cracked open to the outside, chain pulled tight. From the bed, stars glinted through a still creased curtain accidentally left open by an elbow or shoe. On the street, on a pay phone, a passerby stared. Her hair and skirt pocket familiar. She became flowers, then me, then child. And I am watching her watching me.

I am watching a woman pull her own child from her body. We are folding into her. She watches the child at my breast from the screen, from the street, from two towns over my own mother, lips rosed and eye sharp, turns to look. On a patch of brown folding to green surrounded by Naked Ladies, austere and leafless and foreboding, as though the future has been seen and spoken, woman and child, woman and child, woman and child.

Imagine a God

After Joan Mitchell's Cross Section of a Bridge, *1951*

Imagine you are halfway to something
like gravel suspended in the shallows
of a stalled waterway. Imagine a bridge.
Imagine a deer roadside. Imagine a hen trapped
inside a scaled mass that constricts
and slacks. Imagine a child waiting

like a leaf or gum wrapper outside a store.
Imagine a god must see creation this way,
as travelers who've forgotten the thrill
of movement, frozen in an always cresting ocean,
always white, always frothing, always
the breath between wax and wane,
always the bend, the winding approach.

We are lights always blinking.

Reciprocal IVF or How To Explain the Similarities Between Ecstasy and Loss

These months, I think God might be woman un-named—
creation unclassified by words. I cannot explain loving
this child
            —she is not mine—
                        or losing what cannot be lost.
I cannot explain how infertility feels in all my small and deep
spaces. I'm not the only mother to carry loss, lament arrival,
mourn acquisition. Like water swirled to mud, like all the gray
evenings remembering orange. I can't explain this sadness
to my wife.
            —carrying what isn't mine—
                        even to myself.
Not even color or sound can explain. No refrain can breathe *oohs*
into the roundness, thick and opaque, nothing can soften the pitch
and frenzy of my motion,
            —she moves inside me—
                        of my ecstasy and loss.
A man in line at a movie theater once told me you can't love
both God and living—human history is one of incompatibility, the Fall
means we are always beetles struggling on our backs.
How wondrous it must be to live for death.
                        —how beautiful—
I cannot explain how it feels to take depths into my body,
to become—held by her hands soft from never having said *I'm sorry*—
to spin without breaking, to give every word to the world,
to swell and swell and swell and stitch it all together at Her feet.

IVF Egg Retrieval

Later, we will imagine the children, latchkey, weeping
into a dish that sustains them. Some will die. We are all
pro-choice, the doctor, the nurse, my wife. It is never discussed.

How else to watch what wants to divide? How else
to take the want from my wife's body? Later, we will ask
if we ought to mourn the lost. We imagine them like fish, flushed

or buried by the children, the two already born, next to our
side yard sapling, marked with brown-tipped roses from the bush
by the garage. This is the dead we've buried together. Later,

my wife will swear a lot. Anesthesia. The nurse is an ex-Marine.
My wife, Army. Everyone will laugh. Later, in the hotel,
she will lay her body naked against my back. Our room,

across from the hotel pool, filled with the screams of children.
How else to wait and mourn? Her skin damp, the slow
press and grind of her pelvis against the soft of my legs.

By Four Months Pregnant, Surging Hormones and Lack of Sleep
Disturb Cognition, Brain Circuitry, and Spatial Memory

These are the silent days. Is there a word for the emptiness of another person
growing each day inside, how each growing ounce erodes another piece?

That word must be something like the sound of a finger plucking itself
across a fretboard from chord to chord. These silent days, without words,

are like the sorrow of the resurrected at seeing their beloved again, wordless
and familiar, as numbness spreading across a fresh red cheek, as numbness

spreading in a child's chest after learning aging means not every fear
will be comforted. As stories turn to humming, the silent days fill

and fill themselves. No word exists to explain how one thing is two, the joy
and the pain of every slow and pulling end, for mothers this is true. The leaves

are changing, no more beautiful than before, yet a season for speaking.
Dust lifts and rolls from the fields in an unseen breeze.

Season 7, Episode 15: "Kardashian Therapy, Part 1"

My ex-wife is standing between us. A boulder, a ravine, a mist of brick and stone; I can't touch your face even when you're inside me. Hard to tell if it is hormones or a guilt I've contracted like a fever, without warning: deep crimson and flushing. In fact, her words speak from your mouth. Hard to hear. My ears melt and drip to the floor. I was the problem all along.

When we met, you must have thought this obsession with words cute. Like fifty-year-old men in the arms of twenty-year-old painters or dancers or potters. Women are expected to grow up—shed their kitten fur—as all wives do. Aren't we so exciting, stuck and still in the moment when dreams make a woman interesting? Now I am danger. I'll write about the shallow bowl of your hips, how the stink of your ears is sweet and familiar as milk: the danger of living in a mirror written by someone else.

I'm trying here, with each word, to throw out all that I have kept, everything I held in my dark and roomy closets.

The Wordless: The Unspoken and Unnamed

At six months pregnant, the limits of language make me cry
over every sound: all the lowing cellos—sounds strung up

on laundry lines, displayed like underwear flapping itself crisp
and unopening, how the bow moves like wind across strings—

every tinny brass—beaten into my palms, stalled and toed
up my arms. I don't play an instrument, so I'm missing

words to explain how every sound feels, how it feels
to grow another woman inside me, how to explain God—mostly that—

and the child with my hair and eyes I'll never someday have. How
can *sadness* mean all this? The words, nameless as the Water-Drawers,

the Damsels, the 10 Concubines of David—all the unworded women,
unmouthed and untongued mothers and daughters. Some word must

exist to give language to all the women who exist only in the sigh and struggle—
the shuffle on of boots in lingering lines—all those lost to silence.

I point to the leaves' motion in a tall and muted wind;

I tell my new baby to watch their flutter. I list all the things I know that flap—mostly in flight. We can't feel the breeze from the porch. Her neck is sour. Her nails sharp. As it should be. I'd like to tell you the moment ends, nothing painful waits beneath the skin. I'd like to be someone who sees mostly joy—some are. Even the wasp and paralyzed hopper belong—watch yourself, not everything's an omen, but here you're right—even in the morning, even on the silent wind, heavy with honeysuckle, refracting sweetness off every pore on our bodies: If I leave in the night, what will she remember of my mouth and hands? What of my body or blood lingers inside hers?

How to Explain Infertility When an Acquaintance Asks Casually:
After Joan Mitchell's Low Water, *1969*

Think about what is green in green,
how words like *silver* and *bright*
sing off every stinging tight space.
I eat. I sit. I repeat. All must have
order. Line up the shoes. Organize
the bottles.
              Remember how some women
drive their cars off cliffs into ravining water,
children asleep, full and snug and shining
in the trunk? These women, on these days,
gold and glittering, must rejoice in flight; air rushes
their lungs, a chorus of women and falling and clattering
metal sings all together. Water cascades and rises,
foretells all the women and children dead,
a history of female drowning.

Those are not your women.
                            Think of the green
in green, the color that rests just beyond your fingers,
inside, like dirt trapped under grass, like garlic
sprouting, like a long dead bone turned to rock,
tumbled through pulsing years, its ridges and bumps
pressing your flesh, all the small plunges.

Water cascades and rises, foretells all women and children.
Spatter and spray cling but eventually disappear.
How terrible it is
                    to release something from your body.

Keeping Up

I'm in love with the idea of my wife, my ex-wife, all of my exes too, really—porcelain dolls tied together with string, their heads knackering together in my attic boxes. I don't want to be the type of woman who lives only in sadness, but we don't pick which type we are.

Sometimes, I bite the baby's hang nails when no one is looking, swallow her, try to return her body to me. I'm in love with the Kardashians because they will never die.

Sometimes, I see rot and bone when I look at the baby in my arms. How grotesque it is to live in our flesh. I'm in love with the flawless screen, with flashing teeth.

Season 10, Episode 6: "Don't Panic!"
After Anselm Kiefer's Zim Zum, *1990*

I'm watching a woman. I'm watching a man take her picture. She stands still. Sprayed. Teased and tousled. He moves fast. This way, that. *Do a lot of women hate you?* She is watching me watch her, baby at my breast. Not her really. Not the her inside the mouth, behind the teeth. They are so white.

For weeks after the baby was born, I wanted my wife near, proud to display us: stuffed and silent as game, as dinner, as things painted and posed—cadavers—but that may be taking things too far. Now the walls are doing what they must—closing and crumbling. I'm struggling to keep up, pushing my face into stone. *When I come home, will you have hurt the baby?*

I'm watching a woman. I imagine her white teeth biting into the flesh on my smooth inner arm—almost baby fat new. I imagine how she must look prostrate under a sheet—I do mean hands and knees. Even a woman thinks this. The slow work teeth can make of clothing. Years ago, a woman fell asleep drunk between my legs. We laughed in the morning. I'm watching a woman. She is naked, pregnant. Does this change how you feel?

After the baby, I needed another person to mark me valuable. You've seen it in the movies. But on the screen, a man in the distance needs only a sandstone colored hat to prove his worth. Now, as if the screen has tipped, spilling seeds into that cupped and waiting void, my hands fill and fill and fill. I can't keep up. I should tell someone that each night when the baby wakes, I hear my mother's voice cry out my name.

On the days I think about my stay

in a mental hospital, my children say *Mom,*
and the word thorns under the skin on my face,
stings, swarms my ears. Today, they shoot
bubble guns into tall grass. Bubbles
skim the feathered stalks, burst in a drainage ditch.

All of this, precious—the neighbor tilling,
dark birds circling, children's distant screams—
brightness pours from every chest, even the birds
are good—feathers stick to our feet like vanilla,
we are all blinded by the rising light. On these days,

their lullaby voices tug at the fibers of my lasting
grief. Even the birds know what is waiting to open inside
these children's glassy bodies, waiting to cleave itself

from their skin, waiting to stitch all their jagged pieces.

How to Come of Age

Rather than let blood from labia, inner arm or thigh—ritual separation of skin—let me become plainly, as a story: A girl and a man. This story has never been told. This story is told every day.

Woman knows the story as memory, doubts all the years between, doubts the granite beneath her fingers, the child tugging at her hem. Woman remembers the man's warm hand, how his fingers and palm formed a bowl he poured her still hairless body into. His body was warm beneath her and around her. Woman remembers the shape of her brother lost in the glow of a screen before them; her mouth is screaming, her mouth never opens, her mouth doesn't even breathe.

This is the scream all women learn, the sound only we hear, only in remembering, only after years have changed warmth and flesh, whisper and beat, to piercing silence—only women can hear this pulse. The child in this story learned the wordless scream in the man's basement, on the man's lap.

I can't look at my daughters without feeling his hand move between my legs.

Slowly/Suddenly

"The most common symptoms of MS include fatigue, numbness and tingling, blurred vision, double vision, weakness, poor coordination, imbalance, pain, depression and problems with memory and concentration. Less commonly MS may cause tremor, paralysis and blindness."
—The National MS Society

I won't sleep for the risk of waking. Wrapped in an ever tightening band, I can't stop redefining the word *nostalgia*. After *diagnosis*, every word requires reimagining—how I live in the memory of movement, a fluid swimmer, live in the amazement of first wheel builders. How to explain paralysis that creeps into the calves and thighs and hips? The brain insists nothing can be said on this experience. I'm afraid to sleep. When I wake, I'll remember my body is lying motionless in this bed.

Paresthesia: Heat is sharp. Water is paper. And the weight of you like a blanket on my legs crushes the air from my lungs. Trace your finger up the inside of my thigh. I am wet. Not like before. Not how you think or remember. But the wet of ice in the bath. Coldsuddenblue. The higher you touch, the more anticipation is replaced by fear.

I'm writing a novel in my head. On my hands actually. My left thumb taps out code now. On its own. Independent. I can read dots and dashes now. I know I'll have to translate language for you eventually. This is all going to confuse. I suppose I need to get past that confusion. I'm high on Codeine and Xanax. This isn't an excuse. It's best to be honest. One helps me sit still in this shell, crystalline and lead. The other keeps tears from turning ugly.

Red bird on a whitebone branch: all the branches swing, catch like hairs in a sudden drafting wind—northern, awkward—toward some blankness even I can see from the window. Imagine lying beneath this chaos. How wood moves while rooted in the solid shifting solids beneath you, how everything is frozen but dancing white and glowing, how you might feel your arm reach slowly up and up into some empty space waiting above you.

Like children and waistlines, leaves resist managing, and the parking lot branches are nearly bare. I can't ever remember when leaves are timed to fall. This is the straggling time—worse than the naked brown. I'm embarrassed for the trees. Not for their exposure. What woman could dare refuse empathy for their spreading, how hands creep and slide and dip—persistent into every secret burrow? Stripped by wind and watched by passersby—we know how to imagine that.

In this place, I memorize new refrains. *What is happening to your body isn't happening to your body.* I'm embarrassed by the gratitude of trees. How must it feel to let go over and over? How lucky the bloom and return, the sweet blossom and breeze as if purple and blue were a current of traveling breath looking for home. *I can do anything for fifteen minutes.*

How might fuchsia settle to rest on my open arms? Green—unbreakable green—come to rest in my marrow? Inside this hospital room, I'm embarrassed for gratitude, the grandeur of my hope. In the electric pain, the blackblack center of the pain, is a silence I can't explain to you now. I won't ever know how to say silence, stripped naked in the glass, entered my room.

This is how the numblightning spread from my big toe to my belly, wrapped and caressed my body—slowly and suddenly. I can't explain how I want to put it all in my mouth: the children's fingers—dirt under their nails—my wife's ears—how she hates when I tongue the stink from her neck. Now I shuffle to the car, shuffle down the hall, shuffle to the mail: invisible while everyone looks at me.

Spasticity, you are the love I've always known—how something in living, and living female, tells you this will one day come for you—disaster and the sound of something legged and humming that advances and recedes as liquid on the ground.

I want to join their cult of gratitude. I want my face and teeth and hair to glow with the gratitude other women seem to feel for just not being dead. *It could be worse*, I quip to an acquaintance who can't even bring herself to stop when she asks and brushes by me on the sidewalk.

What I like about murder is the absence of language, to live in the chaos. For a moment—nothing. So I watch only true crime and never leave my bed. No manual or explanation exists for infanticide, any violence done to any body. The family annihilator, the angel of death, the sadist, the blitz. I can be them and not them, put my body in the emotionless body holding the knife, the pick or hatchet—a splintered jar inside a jar.

When the more-famous-than-me-poet asks if I'm pregnant, it is difficult to stop myself from screaming. I smile. I'm only a few weeks walking again without the cane, fifteen pounds heavier from steroids. The brain is meant to scream. If any of you speak and I forget to respond, imagine my scream—silent and piercing as a toddler buckled into a stationary car.

II.

This is why, even with a broken heart, a mother will bring herself back to life.
—Claudia Dey

As I read the text messages on my wife's phone,

I struggle to capture—in a neat, tight box—the heat spreading across my chest. Later, she'll ask if I felt sad at all. My face always looks just angry. To explain how the heart trembles, how an ache seems to swell and swell the longer you push your fingers into the pulsing and liquid center—isn't enough. I try to hold on to her arms

lifting me from my hospital bed. Hold how she adjusted tubing that branched like crags and ravined from my body. My eyes glued tight with salt. How the water etched my checks, dried skin to paper, and she walked backwards holding my body to hers, walked me to the bathroom over and over, washed my hair, called out to nurses on the intercom, spooned broth into my mouth after testing the heat on her tongue. Love is both of us swimming

in an ocean of morphine—both of us reaching out for the other. Love is this other woman too. And we all live in the warm wound of my slowly splintering heart dropping clots like paint in the shallows.

How it Feels to Unravel
After season 13, episode 2: "Paris"

If I can give myself anything, let it be a way into anger. My life breaks my flesh slowly apart, every word a loaded gun with no trigger. Imagine a woman's voice singing like a violin. Imagine the *oh* in the hinge of your knee between cartilage and cap, synovial fluid vibrating. Imagine teeth grinding at night, tires drifting over the sleeper lines, bone against bone the rhythm of unraveling.

Imagine a simple cadence, people begin clapping as if living outside the beat is unbearable, each of us a ripped page. My sternum wants to crack from the cage, to unravel. Push two fingers deep into the breast, try to numb the ache.

One day, my daughters will spoil: my inner voice will become theirs, we will collect our female thoughts together like daisies: *I am ugly. I am flawed.*

Imagine daughter as commodity, something raw. Imagine a factory constructing washers or brads or bearings. Imagine anything manufactured. When my daughters say *yes*, they will not understand. We pass our memories through our bodies and one day their lips will mouth *yes* automatically. Inside all of this slowly parting flesh, I am a mother unraveling.

When you undo the done,

you startle like a tall step, a red sign, a flashing light. Some unbecomes happen slowly—melting ice on granite, the swiftly turn of a hand lifting, bread fresh six days: how mold seems to rise rather than fall to rest and spread. Some unbecomes happen quickly as lace or thin surface water, frozen, scraped to curls.

To unbecome your pain is to become pain, to warm bathe in short breath and the quick shallow beats of your stumbling heart and know every day the pain will come, the car drive away, the door shut, the lid close.

When Glass Breaks, the Cracks Move Faster than 3,000 Miles Per Hour

Once, her son stopped breathing. She saw her arms,
sedate and thick, around his shoulders, felt her own breath
as a burden forcing her into a chair. As a girl,

she knew love was like 10,000 small and desperate boxes,
knew her body, now marble and smooth, would one day
turn jagged and home would feel like stone pressed

too long into the shoulder of a rocky shore. She doesn't know
anything about the human heart but that a lover's smell lingers
in her shirt long after they've left her bed. She watched

a man die once. He reached out his arms as if begging
the room to shrink, as if he wanted her to touch her fingers
to the small hollows of his feet, as if he knew

he had smelled the scent of another person for this one last time.

My New Wife Tells Me She Has Given Enough Patience
After season 2, episode 8: "Kardashian Family Vacation"

Impossible to get out of the car in our driveway, to even pull in or turn down the street. Inside—waiting like water to fall as rain—everything I love. You. The children. Even the laundry. All the inevitability of loss. I love you so much I want to leave you. Before the days become long. Before your laughter curdles. Before our kisses sour. Before I yellow from obligation. This love is like water. The children are shiny, tentacled. I want to abandon them roadside, at the therapist's office, forget, eternally, to pick them up from school. This is both easy and difficult to understand. I've been wrong about so much.

The Crown

Her regrets loom, round and full as the planet. As paper dolls flutter and shirk off their dresses, she too is uncertain. When the softly tufted head appears, she wears the crown as both a cotton slip and a noise, gentle as a moan or sigh. The crown is both an opening and a closing that is stitched as hands together in anger or in prayer. She feels the crown in waves that tighten and tighten: the lift of feathers in motion, carrion waiting like powdered and sequined girls, a ball driven like a skipping stone across artificial grass.

It may help you to imagine the cinema. A camera pans and pans. The image bright and swirling. Sharp faces spin and swim, dive and reappear into background wet with orange and yellow: kitchen, yard, office. As if a lifetime has passed and you, the watcher, felt everything though the spin and song. Remember how the spinning always, as it must, stops.

The camera cuts to a cold and hospital white, the white of ending, of beginning again. The crown is like this. The crown is every in-between space: the soft fade of flesh opening before blood raises itself to surface, earth parting and parting as something ancient and green and liquid presses underneath. The crown is a destination: the air we breathe, the black under our nails, the sleep we fall into. The crown is a silent roar—halfway to speaking—and the beauty of a long and lonely scream.

Moored
After Joan Mitchell's To The Harbormaster, *1957*

I want something slipped between my fingers:
a sliver pen, a glass bottle, ice still tacky, ice before it thinks
about becoming liquid again, ice before it desires a tongue
pressed flat against the curving back.

Becoming a mother has changed my hands. My trembling
hands betray me when I reach. I'm middle aged. I'm sinking.
I no longer belong to a world envious of objects
that never hint at death. Our world shrouds mothers
in waves; mothers wear the water till it thins and tatters
our edges, our skin transparent as nightgowns,
our bodies like a sea of humming bees.

Early Menopause

All birds forget how to fly. Crows and blackbirds
walk through parks and cul-de-sacs on invisible stilts.

All schools chain their doors. Women and girls pray wordlessly
in supermarkets between plastic forks and bottled water.

All breezes stop whistling through the stray hairs
on teenagers' necks. Wind purses lips and blows and blows.

All is silent as a man in a black bowler hat. I watch my children
play at the park. My son shoots a stranger's son with his finger.

A girl drags a small stuffed dog behind her on a leash.
The shot hits his temple. The bang is metal piercing flesh,

a pin striking the casing of a round; the noise
bounces off the spiral slide, picnic tables, grills

enshrined in concrete. I can't explain why the skin folding
between my legs is tight like a scar, why men now brush

against me in crowds as if I am a shudder. I can't explain
how it feels in the bowels, on the teeth, on the still smooth bits

of skin in the pit of my elbow—this is where it stings
and hums when you suddenly disappear.

Poppies
After Joan Mitchell's Untitled *(pastel on paper), 1991*

On and on we go behind semis and tractors
trailing loads of dirt. These few poppies
tucked in a field are our past lovers.
Something about my aging tells me
all the orange punctuating the canvas
has to do with letting go. This must be so.
Let go of alone. I am always alone. Let
go of relief. She is always an itch, an ant on the long hair
at the nape, a single irregular stone in a boot.
This must be so. On and on past field
after speckled field, past rusted combine blades
held on to just in case, past the poppies
that don't belong to this field except
as every old love lives in each wet shudder.

Watching Dust Glow in Window Light
After Joan Mitchell's La Ligne de la Rupture, *1970-1971*

As if the earth has been domed and shaken,
all that shimmers is at once caught.

Daughter, we are floating
in the space between our bodies.
Breathe deep. We breathe together,
and we are dust inside each other.

Every breath you take cracks me.
Every step. I want to keep you safe.
On days I wish you'd never been born,

much of this world is your delicate mouth,
your caged-bird lips
                        trembling for wind.
So much of me drowns in your liquid eyes walking
out our door toward your mother who left you.

After the Inauguration, Everything is Portentous

I think about absolutes of motion when I'm naked,
how a pendulum swings, how a scale unbalanced
must wobble, how my skin ripples, weight unsteadies.

Something alive is buzzing in the kitchen, leg
against leg, string against bow, like the sound
of nothing, boxed and electrified. Blackness

circles the sky above my son's school most afternoons.
I want to say *blackness* as if dawn or waking from sleep
or blood rising to air were sinister, but the feeling

on my skin is more like dust, fine and granular, settling
even in my throat. I could say the circling and flapping
and cawing will alight as sediment, in the corners,

in the morning, after God has closed the eyes,
after God has opened them again. Because my children
don't notice my body unclothed, when I walk naked,

I am emperor. I parade the living room, parade
this boulevard of blind children. The images we steep in
are invisible. On the playground at my son's school

children in puffed and quilted jackets gather and ring
around a solitary boy. The children silent, the boy's mouth
buzzes. All the feathers, dark and rustling, fall from above.

Mother

When she left, I felt the children as grating need: *mom* and *mom* and this and that and look and do. Alone with their need, I clung tight. The daughter was still suckling from her. The daughter's screams were beautiful. They came two or three times every night, a fullness in the empty house—long and thick and bright. Some of those alone days, I'd slip my feet into her shoes, like my father's shoes when I was a girl, run a bag of garbage to the can.

The daughter would not be touched when she screamed. I kept the screams, a dampness on the small of a back, a small stone pressed into the sole of a shoe. Some days, I'd think about killing, remember that dream where I'd murdered someone: a body thumping in my trunk to the rhythm of the road.

The daughter's screams had to scream to silence. The daughter would crawl, wet and tonguing the air, searching. Years later, she returns each month to take the daughter for a visit. I pack the screams in a bag along with lip gloss, two crisp five dollar bills, a small stuffed flamingo. I remember every night I tucked the screams into bed and promised never to leave.

Who's Afraid of Silence?

I want to tell you pain has whispered its silence on my skin: how we once spent an afternoon ripping our fingers into orange flesh over the kitchen sink, pulp and succulent dripping, sweet coating our arms. I'm washing in the still solidliquidsolid sound. How the yellow day shine-light is now so often both cold and alone—*this silence is so loud*—and I lay in our bed and form shapes with my mouth and hands to explain. You were supposed to love me enough to save us. I am stones once held together by your certainty. And one day, I might see me as you have. How terrible.

I wish I had at once known and numbered my dead, anticipated how they would flop to surface gasping. Isn't love meant to love what rots in corners—love the remains unburied.

The Color of Tearing
After Joan Mitchell's Hemlock, *1956*

Some women say red is more ghost
than shadow, more rising than lurking,
welling than draining. Some women
say flies nip at the sweet running edges
of a child's skin opened to breathing
light. Some women say more blue,

always. Red is just memories: a mother
who never returns, a lover's pants
badly creased, the distance between
father and daughter, tinny and coiled.

Some women say blue is screaming
from the mouth, like the sizzle of hairs,
red too sharp, too fast, the lost breath
of running, the crisp hard earth on a back
at landing. Some women say the color of the tear
must be the dark green of a pine: the thump

of a zipper catching, the pied hum of a baby
being born still. Some women want to say being torn
is yellowed separation, like two pages spread
to empty them of spatulas, dust pans, small mossy statues
that fall from inside a once white closed body.
Some want. They spend their wanting like coins.
Some want color like the promises

of gold, a shimmer kissed on the mouth.
Some women know shading, patient
beneath each embrace, know what comes
after, separation and the whisp of clothes
unclinging, electric body unplugging
from the leafy pull of another body.

Some women know: The sky pulls out its hair
at our distance. A mother tries to explain impermanence
to her small child. The sky listens. The sky wants
to fall down on both of them, wrap them
in a tight cold band of breath and water.

A Horse Running

After Joan Mitchell's Faded Air I, *1985*

Call the sunset a horse running:
one object hurls toward another,
downward stamp, hardness collides,
splatters into a pink haze.

Call your own body a horse running:
the slow inverse hump of a back—
how we slow, limp, scrape what builds
and sticks from our angular bones.

Call the planet's ellipse a horse running:
curving patterns both stayed and varied,
vast bodies delighting in motion, delighting
like the patter of my own female heart.

The Actual Size of the Rifts in the Human Heart May Vary
Depending Upon Age and Use
After Joan Mitchell's Untitled, *1959-60*

If you do not experience explosions—flames
like billows falling from tall closet shelves,
something soft in the blue becoming
orange, how almost all of us want to reach
out our fingers, touch the heat as it pillows

from under the skin of a lover—if you do not
experience explosions, then you will not feel
the pull from this attraction, even when a tongue figure eights
in your mouth, on your pelvis, even the slow trace
of your bones draining into the basin of another woman.

I can no longer see love when it's given to me. But the moon,
burning only by the heat of another body, can change color,
can change slate and transparent to fuchsia as smooth
and whorling as sepals opening and opening.

Doorway of the Mother

A mother on fire sits up and smiles through the flames.
I will be with you wherever I go.

A mother under the knife cups nothing in her hands.
You are made of me. You are dawn
and wind and dirt climbing free
from the earth. You are made of me.

A mother squeezes the arms tight, too tight.
I need a minute. Please. Just.
Be quiet. For a minute.

A mother unfolding her hands clenches her teeth.
Some muscle in her body must be tight as horses running.
This is my mouth. This is my brow.
These are my fingers crooked
and ugly at the first knuckles.

A mother tells a stranger that this is not her child—
some are bound to never know where they are going.
You are bluer than the moon.
You are bluer than the river.
You are the best I have ever done.

A mother dances, stomps. A mother
dances like a saxophone taps.
I carry your heart. I've eaten your heart.
I've eaten myself eating your heart. Don't worry.
I gather your tears and eat those too.

A mother was a child once without love. She calls the earth a person.
In the beginning, no one needed to be told how to become a person.
I cannot undress our ending, soften
the panic of loss. If you stand
as evening in forgiveness of the day—
it's like that. It's like that, child.

Tabitha Hears a Drum Beat a Familiar Rhythm in the Distance
After Pablo Picasso's Les Demoiselles d'Avignon, *1907*

I imagine she craved the faces of strangers after and never learned the word *resurrection*. She woke posed and ready for display. *This is not my body raised. My hands and feet washed and spelled, my heart, oh my heart. This is not my body.* She must have needed strangers. Now, we watch strangers' faces as they make love on television, greet each other in airports. Strangers often have the look of our lost and dead. *The people are like rain, life deafening. All the men line up to put their hands on my body, touch my arms and back. This is not my body.* Women must love goodbyes. We wake each morning confused from sleep. Will we be clothed on our day as the room empties of women? When the women finally return, will we hear the city sounds, the drums' beating as regret?

Facebook Suggests I Might Know a Man
After season 6, episode 15: "Kim's Fairytale Wedding"

His hair is long, struggles limply in the small picture, but the name I remember. Hard to forget this first kiss—eleven years old, with tongue—to forget how he pushed me hard against the bricks of his house still covered with raindrops, the grass—unmowed for weeks in fall rains—covered with raindrops. He kissed me hard. His tongue hard. His hand hard as it pressed and pressed hard between my legs. I didn't feel any of it. He's in a wheelchair now. You're wrong—I don't tell you this because it is just or judgement—it is simply so. I'd rather have held the rain close, close as the drops I'd watched run down the blades as if paused on my brother's VCR, held how, after, my sweater pilled in the small space where my upper back pressed hard into brick. Seeing him like this should have made me feel. But nothing is as good as it looks on the screen: hotel room towels, cheeseburgers, politicians. Not even kisses.

Season 11, Episode 7: "Return From Paradise"
After Jasper Johns' Perilous Night, *1982*

My father once opened his chest in the kitchen: his thin glass heart, the stuttering weep from his eyes. Even the neighbors could hear the splinter and groan—this is how grief looks, on a man, in the morning, on a man.

I am watching a man break behind dark sunglasses. He lost his family in a wet clouded night. I imagine his mother once numbered the times her own husband had wept—she told her child every story, counted them on his arms: one, two, three.

What is a child meant to learn? Today at the park, my son refused to drink from a pink plastic cup. How fragile their thirst must make them: drying and cracking under the weight of every brittle swallow.

Say the ocean is fluttering,
After Joan Mitchell's Hudson River Day Line, *1955*

3000 silver wings, small, iridescent, slicked and undulating
like a rumble trapped in a paper box. Say all the trees
are growing fat, greener each moment. Say every train
is powered by alarm, a deep, cold puff of smoke in morning wet.

Say the roadway sleeper lines whisper lullaby and goodnight,
press 7 kisses into palm after palm.   Say the city lost all
roads and grass runs naked, untethered, in and out of theaters
and taverns. Say fried chicken can fly.   Yes,

now you must work hard, as the drumstick, the breast,
coated and delicate are difficult to wish otherwise.
Say all the air is sweet as pennies, all the shoulders
strong as ink, all the flowers pink, soft, wanted.

Say my body, drooping and defiant, is a thing I can possibly control.

The Sound of Begging

In the begging—flounder
and drowning, primordial,
liquidblack, an ocean wail—

I wanted the body saved.
You can imagine
how lovers must feel to live—
not alone but distanced—

just out of reach
from every breath and growl.
In the begging,
nothing human.
Human was love once

without flesh
or fire. You can imagine
the begging as smoke,

as a sticky fog
that lingers on the tongue,
breath exhaled
from a full flesh mouth.

Creed

After Mark 9:24

I believe in the question. The question is a place that breathes bluesmooth. The question breathes from the mouth: lightelectric. I believe in darkness, how the question lives there behind my closed eyelids.

> In every MRI machine, I imagine my body is a coffin. I try to pray but can only remember the Serenity Prayer. I've never been to AA, but *the wisdom to know the difference.* I can feel the contrast metal spread through my body: webbing, bluecream fibers like filament or fringed tendons.

I believe in the machine, in the whir, the yellowswill that thrums and buzzes my bones. I imagine my fillings loosen. I believe my body is the question and creator. Here, in the machine, my body, the question, and you:

> how I love you and how I don't, how we hurry and slow, how we need and the blackblack space between us, in us, and around us. I believe I am small. *Help me overcome my belief.*

Over One Million Acres of the Boreal Forest are Lost to Logging Each Year
After Joan Mitchell's Calvi, 1964

I've misplaced most of the needles, blue and weeping,
in the bottom of my handbag. Still, I can't escape the forest:
How the trees quiver. How the trees heave. How the trees,
clustered and flapping, flock left and right and back again.

Six men in reflective vests peer into a hole. The rocks roadside
in Missouri feel good to me somehow, not blood stained, just red
and bodily. I am alone here with my ex-wife, the woman who left.
My new wife is home with the children. My ex is here
on the road and waiting outside our old home and she is
a memory evaporating, her face a solitary pond drying
and refilling from sunrise to set.
                        I need a mask to quiet my breath
pumping into the dark, the slowly spreading dark like skin
opening to receive or empty itself of her unshakable burdens.
I'm not thinking of her. Deliberately. I'm not thinking
of her as a blackness filling my chest. This is the feeling:
a camera closes in on a woman's face, her head bowed,
her head slowly resigns itself upward as the lens tightens
the distance. Her chin, her eyes, all quickly sharpened, and she shakes
her hair, just a little. The movement may be a twitch
or a breeze. This woman is plain, she is beautiful, and I know her.

I've misplaced most of the foxglove, pink and peeking,
in the back of my closet. Still, I can't escape the forest:
How the flowers startle. How the flowers tremble.
How the fragrance sticks like bitters in the back of my throat.

Regarding the Conversation When We Compared Regrets

A bird somewhere has given up sleep to prove love.
Some moments demand speaking, so we say nothing.
This is true, though often we tell lies. One day, a bird falls
accidentally. I think the birds are women, really. I'll remember
these months as a great unburdening. A bird somewhere sings
me too. I would cry out with them, but the daughter growing
inside me would hear what she is coming to. This child
is declarative, like a sentence ending. Finally.
When birds speak on the subject of mourning, on
what a body has done, can do
                                        I want to say it more
plainly—feathered and blue as down as heather as
a leaf twisting—my daughter is mine. One day, I'll fall.
She may remember the worst of me. A bird somewhere
has given up. These months, I find myself breaking like wet sand.

Acknowledgments

Many thanks to the editors of the following magazines for publishing several of the poems included here:

Anti-Heroin Chic: "As I read my wife's text messages,"
The Coop: A Poetry Cooperative: "Facebook Suggests I Might Know a Man,"
"I point to the leaves' motion in a tall and muted wind;" "When you undo the done," "The Sound of Begging," and "Who's Afraid of Silence?"
Driftwood Press: "Creed"
Glass: A Journal of Poetry: "The Silence of a Window" excerpted now in "Slowly/Suddenly"
Heartland: "Regarding the Conversation When We Compared Regrets"
I-70 Review: "When Glass Breaks, The Cracks Move Faster Than 3,000 Miles Per Hour"
Literary Mama: "Doorway of the Mother"
Mid-American Review: "How to Explain Fertility When an Acquaintance Asks Casually"
The New Verse News: "After the Inauguration, Everything is Portentous"
Midwest Quarterly: "How to Come of Age," "Keeping Up," "Mother," and "Season 7, Episode 15: 'Kardashian Therapy, Pt. 1'"
Nimrod International Journal: "The Actual Size of the Rifts in the Human Heart May Vary Depending on Age and Use," "The Color of Tearing," and "Over One Million Acres of the Boreal Forest Are Lost to Logging Each Year"
Raleigh Review: "Season 10, Episode 6: 'Don't Panic!',' "Season 11, Episode 7: 'Return From Paradise'" and "My New Wife Tells Me She Has Given Enough Patience"
Redheaded Stepchild: "Tabitha Hears a Drum Beat a Familiar Rhythm in the Distance"
Snakeroot: "Keeping Up" and "How to Come of Age"
Solidago Literary Journal: "Poppies"
Toad The Journal: "A Horse Running" and "Moored"
Typishly: "How it Feels to Unravel"
The UCity Review: "How it Feels to Unravel"
Whale Road Review: "Season 4, Episode 11: 'Delivering Baby Mason'"

Several of the poems in this book were included in the chapbooks *A Season for Speaking* (Seven Kitchens Press, 2019), *Letters to Joan* (Lithic Press, 2019), and *Susurration* (Blue Lyra Press, 2019).

This book is dedicated to my teacher, friend, and mentor, Laura Lee Washburn. Thank you for making me a poet. You changed my life, and I'm forever grateful for your support.

I am sincerely grateful for the help and encouragement of many writers and editors. I am deeply indebted to Lynn Melnick. Thank you for your generous attention to these poems. This book would not have been possible without your guidance.

I'm incredibly lucky to have worked with the faculty at Queens. Thank you Sally Keith, Claudia Rankine, Morri Creech, Alan Michael Parker, and Jon Pineda. Sally, your support of my work helped me to keep writing through trauma. I'm grateful to have had your guidance when I needed it most.

Thank you Katherine E. Young, Michelle Hendrixson Miller, Josh Davis, Richard Allen Taylor, Greg Stapp, Julie Ramon, Roland Sodowsky, Chris Anderson, Melissa Fite Johnson, Lori Martin, and Shuly Cawood for reading, editing, and encouraging my work. Michelle, you are my favorite roomie and the heart of many of these poems. Josh, I'm indebted to you. There are no words to describe the debt.

Thank you to Freddy at Vegetarian Alcoholic Press for gracefully shepherding these poems into the world.

Finally, thank you to the love of my life for living through these moments with me. You are the ground where I land and the air holding me together.

CPSIA information can be obtained
at www.ICGtesting.com
Printed in the USA
LVHW090745200821
695690LV00004B/177